Meditation for Beginners: The Complete Guidebook
By Kane Georgiou

Disclaimer: This book is not intended as a substitute for the medical advice of physicians. The reader should regularly consult a physician in matters relating to his/her health, and particularly with respect to any symptoms that may require medical diagnosis or medical attention.

Cover by Kane Georgiou.

GW00726078

Table of Contents

Introduction
Welcome to the wonderful world of Meditation

You have obviously chosen to purchase this book for a reason. You are curious about meditation and you want to see what all of the fuss is about. A friend might have told you that they use mediation as a means of relaxation. Or someone else told you they use mediation to reach a "higher state of consciousness." You might be curious to see if meditation can help you with your daily life.

Then you have come to the right place, my friend. This book will give you a detailed guide into the art of mediation. We will discuss its history and origins as well as its true meaning. We will dispel some of the common "myths" and stereotypes regarding mediation. We will also tell you why meditation is beneficial to your overall health and well being.

We will give you different techniques for mediation and hints to help you get yourself into a daily routine. We will advise you on ways you can overcome obstacles that might prevent you from meditating on a daily basis.

We will discuss how mediation can raise your conscience and your mindfulness, as well as how it can reduce stress. Meditation can change your life in so many ways.

You might also be wondering what are the differences between yoga and meditation. We will discuss both and tell you how they can work hand in hand to lead you to a happier, healthier state of being.

If you've purchased this book, you are definitely intrigued by the concept of mediation. It is obviously more than just a curiosity by now. We can give you everything you need to know about the proper way to meditate.

Everyday life can be extremely stressful. Mediation can help ease your stress while relaxing your body, mind and soul.

What if meditation is against my religious beliefs?

There are many today, that are against the practice of meditation as they believe it opens the mind to another dimension and goes against the teachings of many religions. However, this is not the case. Most forms of religion use some form of mediation in their prayer or rituals, so do not let this discourage you. We will discuss how meditation is used in the various religions later on, but do not let anyone tell you that mediation is evil. Read the book in its entirety and then you can decide for yourself whether or not meditation goes against your personal beliefs. We are pretty sure you will be fairly surprised. Read on, my friends.

Stress and Anxiety

Life in today's high-tech, fast-paced, demanding society can be extremely overwhelming. You may often feel stressed and anxious. You might not be eating or sleeping properly. You feel as though you are constantly on edge. Did you know that stress is one of the leading causes of many health problems?

There are many factors in our lives that can cause us stress. Work, health, family issues, relationships, and the basic struggles of everyday life. Stress can cause immediate short-term effects such as rapid-breathing, sweaty palms, tightness in the chest and tension headaches. But if not treated properly, stress can lead to serious health issues.

Stress can lead to high blood pressure, heart disease, gastrointestinal disorders, autoimmune illnesses, mental issue and sleep disorders, among others. It is important to handle stress is a positive manner and find healthy ways to relieve stress so you can lead a happy and healthy life. It doesn't mean your problems will disappear, but you will be able to cope with them better.

How Meditation Can Help Reduce Stress

As we delve into the book, we will discuss exactly how meditation can help eliminate stress. To put it briefly, mediation can help relax your mind and your body. A simple ten-minute breathing meditation technique can help slow your heart rate and calm your racing thoughts. Meditating when your first awaken in the morning can help keep you relaxed and calm as you face your day. It can help clear your mind so you can better focus on the day ahead. Meditation before sleeping can help clear your mind and relax your body so you can have a restful sleep.

Benefits of Meditation

There are many advantages of meditation. We will discuss them in detail further on, but here are just a few to give you a general idea of how meditation can benefit your lifestyle.

Helps lower blood pressure

Assists in improving the immune system

Decreases anxiety

Sharpens the mind

Induces relaxation

Increases creativity

Boosts overall mood

Promotes happiness

Decrease pain levels

Boosts energy levels

There are many other benefits of meditation, which we will discuss later, but this give you a general idea of why meditation is so important in everyday life.

Types of Meditation

There are many types and techniques for mediation, whether you are a beginner or more experienced. We will discuss the techniques in great detail later in the book, but here are just a few different types of meditation to give you a general idea.

General Types of Meditation

Buddhist Meditation

Hindu Meditation

Chinese Meditation

Christian Meditation

Guided Meditation

Most Popular Meditation Techniques

Transcendental Meditation

Mindfulness Meditation

Chakra Meditation (Yoga)

Metta Meditation

Mantra Meditation

Zen Meditation

Again, these techniques, as well as others, will be discussed in great detail, we will tell you everything you need to know.

Mindfulness Meditation and Loving Kindness Meditation are two very simple forms of meditation that you can incorporate into your everyday life. Mindfulness Meditation can help you focus on the "here and now" and is a great way to fight anxiety and increase your focus. We have devoted an entire chapter to Mindfulness Meditation so you can have a better understanding as to how this type of meditation can benefit your everyday life.

Meditation is not complicated. Anyone can do it. Whether you take a few minutes to start your day or you want to take part a more involved routine, meditation can become an integral part of your everyday life.

So stick around. We are glad you decided to buy our meditation guide. Let us begin a journey together that can change your life for the better.

Chapter One: The Origin of Meditation

Before we dive into the origin of meditation, we need to first fully understand the meaning of meditation. In this chapter we will define the concept of meditation and trace its origins. Meditation has quite an interesting history and there has been a great deal of speculation as to where and when it actually originated.

What is Meditation?

According to Webster's Dictionary to "meditate" means to engage in contemplation or reflection, or to engage in mental exercise (such as concentration on one's breathing in repetition of a manta) for the purpose of reaching a heightened level of spiritual awareness.

Okay, so what exactly is a mantra? And what is spiritual awareness?

What is a mantra?

A mantra is a sound, word or series of words that are chanted or repeated by someone who is meditating or praying. Broken down it can be defined as "Man" or mind and "tra" which means transport. So basically mantra means to transport the mind.

The purpose of a mantra is to allow only positive actions and intentions enter your mind, while at the same time getting rid of all negativity. You can choose your own mantra or you prefer to get an assistance of a huge guru (teacher) in your meditation practice, they may "gift" you with your own personal mantra.

How does a mantra help with meditation?

We will discuss mantras in depth later, but basically, when used in meditation, a mantra can, in simple terms, give you the key you need to unlock the door to your subconscious and allow positive energy enter your life.

Mantras originated in India over 3,000 years and have become a crucial component in the practice of mediation. They may consist of a single word, a phrase or even just a sound. A lot of the mantras used in meditation are still in the original Sanskrit. They can either be chanted aloud or repeated silently, depending on which type of meditation you are using, as well as your personal preference.

It is believed the mantras can aid in subconsciously changing things such as affiliations, habits or impulses. When used properly, mantras can be used to direct life force energy into our minds as well as help us reach our personal level of spiritual weakness. Mantras need to be practiced consistently over the course of several months to reach the desired level of effectiveness.

What is spiritual awareness?

Again, we will discuss this on a much deeper level when later in the book, but for now we will briefly discuss spiritual awareness in relation to meditation.

Spiritual awareness is defined as a process in which we explore our subconscious in order to become "whole." It is a means of reuniting our physical bodies with our subconscious (or soul or spirit, all are interchangeable). Spiritual awareness can also be referred to as "spiritual awakening" or "spiritual enlightenment."

Benefits of Spiritual Awareness

Help determine your life purpose

Define a clear sense of morality (right or wrong)

Assist you in practicing compassion, kindness and forgiveness

Reflect on the events of the day

Increase our ability to spend time alone in deep thought and reflection

Gain insight into complex topics or issues

Ability to show empathy toward others

You might be asking how this all relates to meditation. Well, that's very simple. Meditation gives us the ability to relax our bodies while quieting our minds, thus awakening our subconscious self, or our spirit. Meditation helps open up a deeper sense of consciousness, thus spiritual awareness.

If practiced properly, meditation can give you the most intense feeling of peace you have ever experienced. It can help you feel completely relaxed and at ease, relieve stress and anxiety, lower blood pressure, increase your level of focus, open your mind and give you a sense of power and healing.

Lift in today's world is so demanding and can be extremely overwhelming at times. Meditation can be the sea of oasis in the stormy waters of our lives. Meditation has almost become a necessity in today's society. If you have never experienced meditation, you are missing out on one of the best experiences of your life. The art of meditation has so many amazing benefits, which we will discuss in great detail in later chapters. But for now let us give you a little background and insight as to the origins of meditation.

A Brief History On The Origin Of Meditation

As stated in the introduction, meditation has been in existence for centuries and is practiced by many forms of religion and spiritual beliefs. But how and where exactly did meditation originate?

Meditation and Ancient History

Meditation is believed to have originated sometime between 5,000 to 3,500 BCE as archaeologists have discovered wall art in the Indus Valley. It is believed that Shamans even used meditation to have "out of body experiences" or journey to "other worlds" using chants, drums and dance. It has been ascertained that they did this to successfully return their hungers as well as provide healing and bless their tribes.

Meditation and the Middle Ages

Meditation as we know it today has its roots in Ancient India. There are references to modern day meditation found in Indian scriptures from dating over 5,000 years. These scriptures, known as the Vedas, or tantras, are the oldest Indian scriptures in known existence.

It wasn't until, Siddhartha Gautama, the first Buddha, that mediation became a widespread concept throughout the entire Indian culture.

Gautama often left his palace to study mediation with his holy men. He was determined to find absolute truth through the practice of meditation. He left behind a doctrine of meditation which became known as Zen meditation, which can be used by anyone in everyday life. This is otherwise known in Sanskrit as "dharma."

We will discuss Buddhist meditation in depth in a later chapter when we discuss at length the various types of meditation.

As Buddhism began to develop as a religion, it spread to other cultures. It became a huge sensation in East Asia, mainly in China. It wasn't until, Dosho, a Japanese monk, discovered Zen during a visit to China in 653 AD, that meditation becomes popular in Japan. Its popularity grew to new heights in the 8th century, as it slowly began to spread worldwide.

The actual name "meditation" is believed to have gotten its roots in the 12 century. A Latin Monk, Guigo II coined the term "meditatum" which means "to ponder." Meditation was slowly spreading all over the world and became a common practice in many religions, including Judaism, in which it was used as a higher form of prayer. It wasn't until the 18th century, however, that meditation became popular in Western culture.

Meditation and Modern History

In the 18th century, Buddhism spared to the West and was extremely popular among intellectuals. Philosophers such as Voltaire and Schopenhauer were huge supporters of Buddhism and the concept of meditation.

Yoga became a major practice in the 1890's, with roots in Hindu revivalism. Transcendental Meditation, which has its roots in Hindu meditation, became popular in the 1960's. It became increasingly popular in the 1970's and today, meditation is a wide stream concept as it is practiced by many religions, as well as thousands of individuals. We shall later discuss how various religious incorporate meditation into their various belief systems.

So there you have it, a brief description into the meaning and history of meditation. We will be touching on a lot of the topics mentioned in this chapter in greater depth in the next few chapters. In the next chapter we shall discuss why meditation is important in our lives and ways in which meditation can benefit us: spiritually, emotionally and physically.

Chapter Two: Benefits of Meditation

In this chapter we will discuss the physical, emotional, spiritual and mental benefits of meditation. We will also get into how meditation actually works to benefit us in each of these aspects.

Meditation has so many benefits. We briefly touched on these in the introduction. Now we will examine these benefits to help you further understand why meditation is so important in our everyday lives. Some of these may actually overlap, but remember; our bodies are connected, so mediation works in many ways to help our bodies run smoother so we can lead healthier, happier, less stressful and more productive and meaningful lives.

Physical Benefits of Meditation

There are many physical benefits of meditation. Let's take a look at some of them in this next section.

- Clears your mind so you can relax and unwind after a hard day at work, or during a stressful situation
- Helps you fall asleep quicker and easier
- Works to stimulate your parasympathetic nervous system

- This is the branch of your peripheral nervous system. Essentially this helps your body and mind return to a relaxed state after you have escaped from the possibility or threat of danger. It returns your body to a calm state after experience stressors in your daily life. Once this system is activated, your body has time to repair and rejuvenate itself safely and naturally. This can eliminate the need for anxiety meds and other harmful substances.
- Boosts the immune system
- Meditation will slow the production of the cortisol, which is the stress hormone. This can greatly boost your immune system to help you better fight disease and infections.
- Improves athletic ability and performance
- Meditation can help refine your ability to focus on a specific goal or event. This is referred to as visitation in the practice of meditation.
- Slows down your respiration
- As you meditate you are focusing on your breathing. This will help slow down your respiratory and circulatory systems, as well as your heart rate. This is beneficial after an intense workout or an extremely stressful situation.
- Helps ease arthritis pain

Meditation can help the body drastically reduce pain levels. And even in instances where it cannot fully eliminate pain, it can help reduce the amount of fatigue and stress experienced by those who suffer from rheumatoid arthritis.

- Can help reduce the duration of the cold and flu symptoms
Studies have indicated that those who regularly practice meditation are less likely to miss extended periods of time from work or school due to acute respiratory issues. It is also believed that meditation can greatly help reduce the severity of cold and flu systems as well as shorten the duration. Some believe that in boosting our immune systems, it can help prevent us from becoming susceptible to colds in the first place.
- Reduces blood sugar levels in those with diabetes
- Lowers blood pressure
- Lowers the risk of heart disease
- Reduces the risk of infectious diseases
- Increases circulation
- Helps slow the aging process
- Increases energy levels
- Lessens the severity of inflammatory disorders
- Helps reduce asthma symptoms
- Can reduce PMS, perimenopausal and menopausal symptoms in females

- Decrease pain from tension headaches
- Can help heal and prevent ulcers
- Helps Reduce muscle and joint pain, especially after physical stress (ie workouts)
- Helps speed up your metabolism and can drastically help with weight loss

Mental and Emotional Benefits of Meditation

- Can assist in lowering anxiety
- Helps sharpen intuition
- Increases levels of creativity
- Sharpens the mind
- Increases happiness
- Helps you gain clarity
- Helps achieve peace of mind
- Reduces depression
- Improves critical thinking for better decision making
- Helps you eliminate and break unhealthy habits (ie: smoking, drinking, etc)
- Helps you stay in the moment
- Helps you control your thoughts
- Drastically increases your attention span

- Improves cognitive brain functioning
- Enables the body to more fully appreciate art and beauty
- Can increase your ability to appreciate and understand music
- Raises levels of compassion and empathy towards others
- Makes you appreciate the world around you more
- Helps you to better enjoy the "little things" in life
- Helps fight postpartum depression
- Improves memory
- Helps alleviate mental distractions
- Helps you reach a state of nirvana (enlightenment)
- Helps curb impulsive and irrational behaviors
- Can enhance self-awareness
- Improves self esteem
- Can help manage ADD/ADHD
- Can help manage and control obsessive-compulsive behaviors
- Heightens our intuition

There are many, many benefits of meditation, as you can see by the above lists. Of course, for those who are serious about meditation, the ultimate goal is to achieve absolute enlightenment, or nirvana. Allow us to discuss this in great detail later on in the book.

But as you can see, meditation is helpful for so many reasons. We will not bore you (or confuse you) with the exact science of how meditation affects the body and the brain. But we will sum it up for you as easily as possible.

How does meditation affect the brain?

There has been a lot of study over the years as how meditation affects the brain. We have briefly listed some of these effects earlier, but now we will touch on some of the effects that have been scientifically proven and studied over the years.
Meditation May Help "Quiet" Your Brain

Meditation can affect the area of the brain which regulates memory and learning as well as areas that affect emotional. Essentially, it has been proven that meditation can help reduce the "volume" of the brain by reducing fear, stress and anxiety. It relaxes those specific areas of the brain in a sense "quieting" them to improve overall mood and well-being.

Meditation Drastically Improve Levels of Concentration

Studies have proven that with just a few weeks of meditation, subjects were able to concentrate on a specific task for longer periods of time. Since one of the goals of many forms of meditation is to focus on one specific object or thought for an extended period of time, this process has been proven to drastically improve the thought process and levels of concentration in both students and adults.

Meditation Can Reduce Anxiety (including social anxiety)

Research has proven that mindfulness meditation in particular, can reduce stress and anxiety, including social anxiety, in those who practice regular meditation. This is due to the fact that meditation affects those areas of the brain which focus on "me-centered" thoughts, thus teaching the mind to reduce, or even completely eliminate those self-regulated thoughts that produce tension and anxiety.

Meditation Can Help Those Suffering From Addictions

Mindfulness Meditation is also believed to be extremely beneficial in helping both treat and overcome additions. It is believed that mindfulness meditation helps eliminate the need for the craving as you are essentially "retraining" your brain to survive without the addiction.

Meditation Can Help Reduce Depression

Mindfulness Meditation is also proven to help greatly reduce depression. It has been proven that those who meditate regularly have had decreased levels of depression and anxiety. Mindfulness meditation calms the brain and helps take the focus off the underlying subconscious factors that are causing depression. It helps teach the mind to refocus and find new and creative ways to deal with everyday situations that can trigger depression and anxiety.

How does meditation affect the body?

Meditation can also help the body as well. Studies have proven that meditation can help eliminate stress, fight disease, ease muscle tension, improved heart and lung health and even lower blood pressure. Since our bodies and our minds are connected, it only makes sense that meditation can help improve the body as well as the minds.

Meditation Can Help Reduce Stress

Not only can meditation help reduce the effects of stress on the brain, but on the body as well. Stress can cause physical issues such as gastrointestinal issues and other health issues. Meditation can help the body feel more relaxed thus helping to reduce the physical ailments from stress, anxiety and depression. Meditation can help calm your breathing during an anxiety attack and can also help your body to relax so you can sleep more peacefully at night.

Meditation Can Help Improve Heart Health

In a study by the American Heart Association, it is reported that mediation helped decrease the thickness of the arterial walls which lowers the risk of stroke and heart attack.

Meditation Can Reduce Muscle Tension

As you meditate and focus your attention on different areas of the body through controlled breathing, your muscles will begin to relax. Studies have shown that athletes who practice meditation have less injuries and muscle tension than those who do not meditate.

Meditation Can Boost Your Immune System

Meditation can boost the immune system by increasing the level of antibodies to fight disease. A study has indicated that those who meditate regularly have stronger immune systems and are less likely to develop colds, allergies and stomach illnesses.

Meditation Can Help Lower Blood Pressure

Meditation and controlled breathing increase the production of nitric oxide which reduces blood pressure by opening up constricted blood vessels.

As you can see, there are numerous benefits of meditation. It can help our body, minds and souls. Meditation can change our lives if we make it a daily part of our lives and practice it on a consistent basis. The benefits of meditation only show how important meditation is to live a happy, full and balanced life. Our minds, bodies and souls can be at one and live in peace and harmony.

In the next chapter we shall give a brief introduction and history of the most popular types of meditation, as well as a quick how to guide on how to practice each. Remember, not all forms of meditation are meant for everyone. Use this brief guide to help you select the form of meditation that best fits your personal needs, beliefs and lifestyle.

Chapter Three: Types of Meditation and How to Practice Each

In this chapter, we will take a close look at the different types of meditation and go into extensive detail as to how to practice each. You can mix and match types of meditation, or simply choose which one works best for you. Remember, everyone is different so what works for someone else (i.e. friend, coworker, relative) may not work for you.

In the next chapter we will give you suggestions on how to prepare for meditation as well as how to overcome the obstacles and distractions that might interfere with your meditation routine. We will also give you suggestions on how to incorporate meditation into your daily routine.

You should make sure to wear comfortable, loose clothing. You should not wear anything that is binding and restricting. You want to be as comfortable as you can. Also, do not get discouraged if you have trouble concentrating at first. Meditation takes practice, as well as patience. In a later chapter we will discuss the various obstacles and distractions you may face during meditation and how to overcome them. But please don't get discouraged if you can't get it down immediately. Everyone is different, so do not judge yourself by others (ever!). Your experience and journey with meditation is unique and personal. The more you practice the better you will become!

Buddhist Meditation

Buddhist meditation is based on techniques that encourage, develop and fine tune clarity, concentration, focus, positive emotions and a sense of overwhelming peacefulness and calmness. There are many forms and variations of Buddhist Meditation, but for the purposes of this book (and so as not to overwhelm you); we will discuss the four most popular forms of Buddhist meditation: Zen Meditation, Vipassana Meditation, Mindfulness Meditation and Metta Meditation (otherwise known as Loving Kindness Meditation).

Zen Meditation (Zazen)

Zen, or Zazen, meditation is translated as "seated meditation" and originated in Japan, although it has its roots in Chinese Zen Buddhism, which dates back to the sixth century. Zen meditation is a very sobering and relaxing meditation technique. There are many places worldwide that have centers and classes on Zen meditation, as it is most commonly practiced as a group activity. However, this does not mean that you cannot practice Zen meditation in the privacy of your own home. A lot of emphasis is placed on proper posture as it is crucial in concentration.

It is important for us to point out that you should not put yourself in any position that causes you chronic pain. If you have health limitations, do not attempt some of the more difficult positions. If you have any questions, you can always consult your physician before attempting any yoga or meditation position.

How to Practice Zen Meditation

Use a mat or small pillow

Get into the proper position

You can choose from one of the following positions. Find which works best for you. You need to feel completely at ease or you will not be able to fully concentrate.

Half Lotus Position: This is also referred to as the "Hankafuza position". You will place your left foot onto your right thigh, and then tuck your right leg under your left thigh.

Full Lotus Position: This position is also called the "Kekkafuza position" and is considered to be the most stable position for maximum focus and concentration. You will position each foot on the opposing thigh. This can be slightly uncomfortable at first but the more you do it, the easier and more comfortable it will become.

Burmese Position: This is by far the easiest of the various Zen positions. Simply cross your legs and rest both knees flat on the floor, with one ankle in front of the other, rather than above. Kneeling Position: This position is also referred to as the "Seiza position." In this position you will kneel forward with your hips resting on your ankles.

Standing Position: This position is most commonly practiced in China and Korea, and is recommended for those who cannot sit for extended periods of time. Stand up straight and tall; your feet should be shoulder-length apart and do not lock your knees. Keep your heels together and place your hands over your belly, with your right hand over your left.

Chair Position: It is totally acceptable to sit in a chair if you prefer. Just remember to sit up tall, with your back straight.

Fold your hands into the proper position

This is known as the "cosmic mudra." Hold your non-dominant hand in your dominate hand, both facing palm up with your thumbs touching lightly.

Close your eyes

Clear your mind and focus only on your breathing

Inhale and exhale, counting until you get to ten

Once you are successfully able to count to ten without any distraction, you need to focus on breathing without counting. This will get easier as you practice.

Open your eyes and warm up your legs and arms

This will return your blood circulation to normal

Mediate for 15-45 minutes

You can start at 5 minutes and then gradually work your way up to 45 minutes

Let your subconscious take over

Zen meditation goes deeper than just sitting quietly. If done properly, it can take you to hidden spiritual awareness deep in your subconscious. This last step is accomplished by letting your subconscious take over by exploring the "stillness" you have created. Use this time to focus on your and the world around you, let your senses take over.

The key to Zen meditation is in the mindset. This will naturally emerge from a deep state of concentration on breathing and posture. It is normally for you to experience images and thoughts during Zen meditation, as well as feel emotions, from your subconscious. Do not let them overpower you, while at the same time you should not ignore them. Simply acknowledge them, but then return your focus back to your posture and breathing.

If you are having trouble focusing, there is a variation of Zen meditation called "Shikantaza" which translates as "just sitting." If you do not have a subject, or object, in mind for your particular meditation, you can just still sit and remain in the moment, taking in your surroundings and allowing yourself to feel and think about things naturally. This method is known to be very calm and relaxing for those who are suffering from severe bouts of depression or anxiety.

Vipassana Meditation

"Vipassana" is translated from Pali as "insight" or "clear-seeing." Vipassana Meditation dates back to the 6th century and is a method used to purify the mind from anxiety, physical and emotional pain, and distress. In this meditation practice, as with Zen meditation, you are not trying to invoke the help of a spirit or guide, but rely solely on your own efforts. The purpose of Vipassana Meditation is to see things as they really are, not as how we perceive or interpret them in our minds. It is essentially a method of self transformation via self-observation and self-realization. It helps us gain a deep connectivity between our bodies and minds to result in a balanced mind that is not only self-aware, but full of love, empathy and compassion for the world around us.

Types of Vipassana Meditation

Kayanupassana

Kayanupassana is defined as "meditation of the body." It focuses a great deal on breathing and getting in touch with our bodies. In this form of meditation, we are focusing on what happens to our bodies as we are breathing such as the movement of our abdomen as we inhale and exhale, the various sensations we are experiencing at that moment, etc.

You will focus on long versus short breaths and how each makes you feel. The purpose of Kayanupassana is to come to the realisation that everything in life is temporary and constantly changing. Suffering, pain, anxiety, etc are all fleeting and shall pass.

Vedananupassana

Vedananupassana is defined as the "mindfulness of feelings." In this type of meditation, you will acknowledge and accept your feelings of negativity, displeasure, etc and ultimately, you will be able to move beyond these feelings and achieve a state of peacefulness, no matter what is happening in the world around you. You will be able to accept the world you live in, without letting it take control of your life.

Cittanupassana

Cittanupassana is defined as the "mindfulness of the state of mind" (or consciousness). Essentially, this practice teaches us to be aware of what is happening in our minds as it is happening, ie: the awakening and intensifying or our desires, our thought processes, and so forth. The ultimate goal of this form of meditation is to see the mind as a series of mental events and processes, as a separate entity from our bodies.

Dhammanupassana

Dhammanupassana is defined as "mindfulness of mental objects" (or phenomena). In this practice, you would focus on the five "mental hindrances": anger, lust, greed, doubt, and sloth and how we can overcome them to achieve peace of mind as well as how our senses reacted to these hindrances.

The main goal of Vipassana Meditation is to attain complete freedom from existential suffering by keeping the mind fully alert, clear and balanced at all times.

If you find this type of meditation a bit intimidating, don't worry. There are plenty of other types of meditation out there. The next one we shall touch on briefly is Mindfulness Meditation, which is in essence, similar to Vipassana Meditation, as it teaches us to live fully in the moment, but it is much less intense. Again, this purpose of this chapter is to give a brief guideline to the basic types of meditation.

However, we feel that as mindfulness is the ultimate goal of all forms of meditation, that we should dedicate an entire chapter to Mindfulness, so don't feel overwhelmed. As we have pointed out, everyone is different and not every form of meditation will work for you. The purpose of this eBook is to give you an overview and better understanding of meditation, as well as to find out which type of meditation works best for you

Mindfulness Meditation

Mindfulness meditation is defined as the "practice of focusing one's attention on the external and internal events of the present moment. It helps us to be nonjudgmental in the way we every aspect of our experiences. Instead of avoiding things, we are able to handle them by just letting them happen.

It helps us to be able to accept that there are some things that are ultimately beyond our control. It also helps us to experience mindfulness is joyous moments and experiences as well. Quite often we ruin a good moment by letting worry and anxiety take over. We are often afraid that this moment of serenity will not last, so we tend to let negativity take over and thus lose the pleasure of the moment.

Mindfulness meditation can enable us to live fully in the moment and experience every situation we encounter throughout our daily lives in a peaceful and serene manner, rather than overcome with stress, worry, angst and anxiety.

The purpose of mindfulness meditation is not to change us in any way, or distract from our true selves, but to enable us to be able to experience every moment to the fullest. When are "mindful" we are "present" in our lives. We do not miss moments or opportunities by being distracted by worry, fear, anxiety, etc nor do we "daydream" the moment away.

We want to be fully aware and present in every moment of our day every day of our lives. Of course, we are not going to reach a state of mindfulness overnight, it will take time to achieve this state. It will take some practice, but ultimately, mindfulness meditation can be an enlightening experience in and of itself as we will be able to experience our lives to the best of our ability.

Mindfulness meditation is also believed to help us gain insight and perspective. As we are living more in the moment, our minds are free and not heavy with worry, anxiety and other factors that take away our peace of mind and ability to focus. Thus, our minds are open and we are able to gain new insights. Our senses will also be heightened as we reach a mindful state. We will be able to fully experience our senses. Ultimately things will taste and smell better, we will experience feelings on a deeper level and so forth. We will learn to truly appreciate every moment of our lives when we learn to live in the present and not be weighed down by the ghosts of our past or fear of the future.

Mindfulness Meditation is helpful for those who suffer from depression, anxiety, ADD, ADHD, OCD and other such ailments. Mindfulness is such a crucial part of our lives that we have actually devoted an entire chapter of this book to it. In this section, we will give you a general idea on how to practice Mindfulness Meditation, but we shall discuss this concept in great detail in Chapter Four. Mindfulness meditation goes beyond simply meditating for ten to thirty minutes a day. It can be applied to how we interact with others, our diet, the way we view things, and so forth. Again, the following is a general guide, but we shall dive into mindfulness meditation and how to apply it to our daily lives in the next chapter.

How to Practice Mindfulness Meditation

Choose a Location

Set aside a time and a place where you will not be distracted or interrupted. You can find a quiet room in your home (or office) or a peaceful outdoor location, such as under a tree or by a lake or near the ocean. A lot of people set aside a specific room or location solely for the purpose of meditation. Find a place that works best for you, one where you will feel safe, secure and comfortable.

Make Yourself Comfortable

Find a position that works best for you. You may use one of the positions we have discussed above, or you may find one that works best for you. Mindfulness meditation is very personal, and a bit more relaxed than other forms of meditation. Just make sure that you are comfortable and not tense, as this will distract you from being mindful and living in the moment.

Take Several Deep Breaths

Breathe in and out several times, slowly. You don't want to inhale or exhale too quickly, as this can make you dizzy as well. Each breath should be a little longer than the previous one. You might need to count at first, but as you become more experienced, mindfulness meditation breathing will become second nature.

Clear Your Mind

Don't worry if you find this hard to do at first. It is not easy for some of us to fully clear our minds and become detached from the world around us. It takes practice. If you are having trouble, take a few more deep breaths or perhaps switch your position. In time, you will find what works best for you.

Focus on the Present

This too, will take some practice. You will find your mind wandering, but you need to keep pulling your thoughts back to the present moment. Let your senses take over: What do you see? Smell? Hear? Feel? Surrender yourself completely to the moment. Experience everything as it is happening in that exact second.

The ultimate goal of mindfulness meditation is to be able to apply it to everyday life. To be mindful in every single moment, this will take time, but setting aside a few minutes a day to practice mindfulness meditation is a great place to start. Again, we feel it is so important that we have devoted an entire chapter to this practice, so stay tuned!

Metta Meditation or "Loving Kindness Meditation"

Metta Meditation, more commonly known as "loving kindness meditation" is another form of Buddhist meditation that involves developing compassion and love.

Even though it has its roots in Buddhism, it is widely practiced by many, regardless of religious practice or preference. It focuses on concern, care, friendship, love, compassion, empathy and kindness. The goal of Metta Meditation is to achieve a higher level of kindness and pure love, from a complete selfless place.

Metta meditation aims to help us breakdown the barriers we hold against ourselves and others. It helps us soften our hearts and open our minds. It teaches us to experience unconditional love for ourselves and others and let go of any prejudices or limitations we might have: whether conscious or unconscious.

Metta meditation is the ability to recognize that are beings are capable of feelings as well as the ability to feel empathy for others and to wish them well. It is designed to bring us a sense of solidarity, or "oneness" with the world around us, and those we come in contact with on a daily basis. Metta meditation can help us achieve the goal of complete emotional fulfillment, a state in which we will be able to share this love and compassion with everyone around us.

There are many types of Metta Meditation. However, for the purpose of this eBook, we will give you a simple guide to practicing Metta Meditation. As well, there are many ways in which you can "direct" Metta Meditation. You can choose to make the "object" of metta meditation either yourself, a specific person, or even a group of people.

Self Loving Kindness Meditation

We are our toughest critics. We often beat ourselves up and tear ourselves down for things that are often beyond our control. Practicing Metta Meditation on ourselves is perhaps the best form of "self-help" that is available, and best of it, it doesn't cost anything!

A lot of people believe that self metta meditation is selfish. Buddha himself said that no one is more worthy of Metta meditation than ourselves. After all, how can we love anyone else if we don't first love ourselves?

Metta Meditation can help us learn to love and accept ourselves; complete with our flaws and limitations. Remember, what we view as a "flaw" someone else might see as one of our best features or characteristics. "Beauty is in the eye of the beholder." Yes, that statement might seem cliché and even a bit trite, but it is true.

We need to learn to fully love, appreciate and accept ourselves before we can feel any love towards others. How can we love and accept someone else if we are bitter, spiteful, hateful and self-deprecating? Metta meditation can help us to overcome the self-doubts, negativity and insecurity that our holding us back from becoming the person we want to be and living the destiny we are meant to live.

Metta Meditation for Others

Metta Meditation may be directed towards an individual or a group of individuals. It may be a family member, friend or loved one. It could be directed toward a group of people with whom you feel empathy or compassion, or wish to feel empathy or compassion. It can be directed toward a person (or group of people) to whom you feel a sense of gratitude. Or toward someone you wish to send "healing energy" or "positive vibes."

On the same token, Metta Meditation can be directed toward someone with whom you feel ill-will or negativity, in order to bring peace and love to both parties. It can help you let go of any anger, resentment or ill-will you feel towards that individual (or group). It can bring a sense of empathy and harmony to both you and the other party (or parties) and reduce and ultimately eliminate any feelings of hatred, bitterness or negativity on either end.

Ultimately, when you direct Loving Kindness Meditation toward someone other than yourself, whether it be a loved one, or an "enemy" (for lack of a better word), your goal is to bring about peace, love, goodwill and harmony to all of those involved. Metta Meditation is designed to be selfless, not selfish.

There are many, many types of Metta meditation, but for the purposes of this book, we shall give you a brief guide on how to practice Loving Kindness Meditation.

How to Practice Metta Meditation

Find a quiet place where you will not be easily distracted

Chose a quiet place in your home, office, or wherever you may be at that moment. Try to find a place where you will not be easily distracted. A quiet room at home, an empty conference room, a favorite place in nature, wherever you feel most comfortable. Choose a position that is most comfortable for you

Metta meditation can be practiced in any of the common meditation, or even yoga, poses or posture. It can be practiced while lying down or in a sitting position. It can even be practiced while standing still or in motion. One of the benefits of Loving Kindness Meditation is that it can be practiced anywhere, as long as you feel comfortable!

Clear Your Mind

Again, you may find this task a bit of a challenge, but it will get easier over time. And you are probably wondering how you will be able to clear your mind when you are experiencing self-hatred, anger or animosity toward another. We will discuss this in depth in Chapter Four when we discuss how to overcome obstacles that might distract us from our daily meditation.

Focus on Your Breathing

Focusing on your breathing technique will help you clear your mind and focus on your mind and body so you can begin your meditation. Remember to inhale and exhale slowly.

Focus on the "subject" of your Metta Meditation

You have probably already chosen the "object" of your Metta Meditation, so at this point, you will take a moment to focus on this person. Allow any negative feelings to dissipate and focus on loving feelings toward that person (or yourself if that may be the case).

Chose you specific phrase

There are many phrases that one can use during Loving Kindness Meditation. You may choose one of the common phrases or you may design on your own. You may start out with a specific phrase in mind, or one may come to you as you are preparing to meditate. Metta Meditation may be something as simple as "May I learn to love myself more fully." "May _____ be well, may _____ be happy, may _____ be free from suffering."

Repeat this phrase over and over.

Repeat the phrase again and again. Allow the words to penetrate your heart, soul and mind. This too, might not come easily at first, it might feel a bit awkward, and you might even feel a bit silly. However, this will decrease the more you practice Metta Meditation.

Your intention is what is important, not the tone or the timing. This will all come in time.

Let the phrase resonate through you. You can choose to repeat it a set number of times, for a set amount of time, or until you feel a sense of peace. This is entirely up to you. Metta Meditation, like all forms of mediation, is extremely personal. Leave yourself open to feel love, compassion and empathy towards your subject

As you repeat your intention, your initial feelings of anger, bitterness, etc should be dissipating and you should be feeling a sense of calm and lovingness toward yourself or your intended subject. Allow yourself to feel love, happiness, compassion, empathy and so forth. Let the positive emotions take over.
Send out feelings of love, empathy, compassion toward the subject of your Metta Meditation

Now that you are experiencing "good" feelings toward yourself or your subject, it is time to "send" these feelings out to them. Allow yourself completely surrender to these feelings of love, empathy, compassion, joy, and so forth. Do not simply "leave them behind" in your place of meditation, carry them with you wherever you go and share them with everyone you encounter.

Hindu Meditation

Hindu meditation is often described as a related state in which one is contemplating or focusing on the present moment. It is also defined as a state of reflection in which the mind is completely free of all thoughts. The goals of hindu meditation can be a complete transformation of energy or attitude as well as spiritual enlightenment. It has also been described as a journey to the deepest part of one's being. In order to achieve this state, one must tap into their inner strength.

It is also believed that if one practices Hindu mediation as part of the morning routine that they will sustain this inner strength and remaining a calm, tranquil state throughout the day. Hindu mediation is used to relieve and ease our "earthly troubles" such as fear, anxiety, doubt and other such negative feelings that may impact our daily lives.

Hindu mediation can be practiced by chanting a mantra, Yoga (which we will discuss in depth in a later chapter), through breathing or meditation on sacred teachings and/or writings. It is believed that this type of mediation will take us beyond our natural state of mind to achieve our full spiritual awakening.

Transcendental Meditation

Transcendental Meditation is one of the most widely practiced forms of meditation. At the current time, there are more than 5 million transcendental meditation practitioners worldwide

A type of mantra meditation, Transcendental Meditation started in 1955 in India by Maharishi Mahesh Yogi. It was extremely popular in the 1960's and 70's. It was so popular that celebrities such as the Beach Boys, the Beatles and others practiced directly under the Maharishi himself.

Transcendental Meditation is taught by certified teachers as a specific cost. Rates for these courses vary by country and program. It is beneficial for relaxation, self development and stress reduction. There has been a lot of debate as to whether Transcendental Meditation is practiced for religious or nonreligious purposes.

It is believed it can be practiced for both, but many hold to the fact that it is in fact, very religious as it is strongly rooted in Hinduism, although those who practice for non-religious purposes stress that the fact that they are utilizing Transcendental Meditation strictly for the purpose of self-development.

Transcendental Meditation is widely used to promote an overall state of relaxed self-awareness as well as a means of getting rid of distracting thoughts. According to those who practice Transcendental Meditation it is a means in which our normal thought process is "transcended" and is replaced by a state of complete, pure consciousness. The goal is to achieve perfect calm, rest, stillness and a total absence of mental boundaries. It has been noted that Transcendental Meditation can reduce anxiety, cholesterol, chronic pain, fatigue, stress and high blood pressure.

How to Practice Transcendental Meditation

As stated earlier, Transcendental Meditation cannot be self-taught. It requires training with a Certified TM practitioner. Most courses are given on a weekly basis, for about 1-2 hours at a time depending on the instructor.

This can be done over the course of a few months or as one intensive program over the course of a week to two weeks. There are also weekend retreats offered at resorts and meditation centers for those who wish to study TM.

The first classes usually consist of an introductory lecture followed by a second lecture in which more specific details are given. Then candidates who are seriously interested in TM will be subject to a personal interview and then 1-2 hours or private instruction in which they are given their personal mantra, which they are told to keep confidential. Next there will be 3 more classes with 1-2 hours of personal instruction in which the teacher will work with the individual on the benefits, techniques and specifics of Transcendental Meditation.

The instructor will meet regularly with the student to ensure they are practicing the proper techniques. It is encouraged to practice Transcendental Meditation for fifteen to twenty minutes twice a day, usually in the morning upon waking and again in the evening before dinner. Transcendental Meditation is not strenuous nor does it require a high level of concretization. Practitioners of TM are instructed to breathe normally and focus only on their mantra.

Mantra Meditation

We touched briefly on mantras earlier. To refresh your memory, a manta is a syllable, phrase or series of words that are repeated to help keep your mind focused. It is not an affirmation to "hypnotise" nor convince yourself of something.

Mantras are used in many traditions and types of meditation including Hindu, Taoism and Buddhism traditions of meditation. It is often referred to as "om meditation" as "om" is one of the most commonly used mantras.

Some practitioners believe that the choice of the word, along with the proper pronunciation, is vital to manta mediation. They say that this is because the vibration is related to the meaning and sound. While others feel that the mantra is simply a tool to focus the mind so the choice of manta is not relevant.

There are many different mantras. If you are studying meditation in a group, or one-on-one, with a practitioner, they may assign a mantra for you. However, if you are practicing meditation on your own you may choose your own mantra.

The main thing is that your mantra is something that is extremely personal to you and vital to your meditation, whatever it may be at that point. You can keep the same mantra forever, or change it as you see fit. Mantras are an extremely personal topic and some believe that you should never share your personal mantra with anyone.

How to Practice Mantra Meditation

Choose Your Mantra
Determine what mantra you wish to use for this particular meditation. You may have different mantras for different intentions or you may use the same mantra for every situation. Again, this is entirely up to you (or you and your instructor if that is the case) and it is extremely private and personal.
Choose an Intention

Determine the subject, theme or focus of your meditation. You do not always have to have a specific intention. It can be as simple as "letting go" or "relax." Again, this is very personal.
Find a Comfortable, Quiet Place

Find a quiet spot in your home or your favorite place in nature. Make sure it is free from distraction and that you will feel safe, secure and comfortable.

Choose Your Position

The most common position for Mantra Meditation is the Lotus Position, but again, this is entirely up to you.

Close Your Eyes and Focus on Your Breathing

Center yourself and clear your mind as you would before any meditation. Close your eyes and focus on your breathing. In Mantra Meditation, breathing is not the main focus as with other forms of meditation, but it does help your clear your mind and get focused before you start your mantra.

Chant Your Mantra

Start to chant your personal mantra. You may want to have a "practice" session first. You might feel silly or self conscious at first, but this will decrease over time. You can set either a number limit or a time limit for your mantra. Most people who practice Mantra Meditation opt for choosing a specific number (most commonly either 108 or 1008 if you are going with traditional Mantra Meditation) You can keep track of your count with beads.

Meditate in Silence

After you have finished chanting your mantra, you may slowly transition into a silent meditation and allow your mind and body to experience any sensations that may occur. You may focus on your intention. When you feel that you are calm, you may stop meditating.

As with any form of meditation, Mantra Meditation will take time, patience and practice, don't get discouraged if takes you some time to "perfect" this form of meditation. Everyone progresses at a different level.

Atma Vichara Meditation (Self Enquiry and "I Am" Meditation)

"Atma Vichara" is the Sanskrit term for "self-enquiry." The purpose of of Atma Vichara Meditation is to discover or investigate your true being. It is essentially practiced to answer the ever-famous question of "Who am I?" This type of meditation will help you find the essence of your true self and provide you with personal and intimate knowledge. It is believed to date back to the 20th century.

Our sense of self (or ego) is the center of our universe. So in essence it is the force that drives our memories, thoughts and emotions. You would think this would give us a clear sense of who we are, however, sadly, this is not the case. Our true sense of self is buried deep within our subconscious and Atma Vichara Meditation can help us dig deep into our subconscious to uncover the mystery of who we really are.

How To Practice Atma VIchara Meditation

You would practice Atma VIchara Meditation as you would any other type of meditation. Find a quiet place where you will not be interrupted or distracted, chose your position, clear your mind and focus on your breathing.

With Self-Enquiry/Atma Vichara Meditation you will focus on the question "Who Am I?" You must use this question simply as a tool to focus on "I am" and reject any verbal answers that come to mind. You must focus deeply on the "I" and become one with it. You are not trying to figure out who you are intellectually, but spiritually. You are trying to get to the core of your subconscious. You must "disassociate" yourself from your environment, your senses, your intellect and your ego.

Self-Equiry Meditation can be practiced anywhere and anytime. Some feel that it is best practiced in nature. It is not something that is easily achieved. It takes patience and practice. You can practice Atma Vichara Meditation at night before you go to sleep or in the morning when you first wake up. You can use it along with yoga or other forms of meditation.

Like Mantra Meditation, Atma Vichara
Meditation is very private and personal and is not something you should share. You can keep a journal if you so desire of your self-journey. It can take several years to uncover the mystery of "Who Am I?" and for some it is a lifelong journey. However, it is the most powerful and meaningful journey of your life and should not be taken lightly.

Yoga

Yoga is a broad term that encompasses many things. We could devote an entire chapter to Yoga, or an entire book even, but we shall touch on Yoga briefly go give you a general idea as to how Yoga is practiced in accordance with Hindu Meditation.

Yoga, or "union," is a practice that dates back to 1700 BC. The goal of yoga is to achieve self-knowledge as well as spiritual purification. Yoga is now perhaps the most popular form of mediation as their yoga classes are being offered with gym memberships, at Health & Wellness Centers, and even Yoga Centers. Weekend Yoga Retreats at remote resorts are quickly becoming a vacation destination as Yoga is taking the world by storm.

There are many different yoga practices and techniques. We shall touch briefly on the most common yoga practices below.

Types of Yoga Meditation

Chakra Meditation

In Chakra Meditation, you would focus on one of the seven chakras of the body (center of energy) while either chanting a mantra or performing a visualization, or both. The seven chakra's are as follows

Root (base) Chakra: the base of your spine

Sacral (naval) Chakra: located between your root chakra and your navel (belly button)

Solar Plexus Chakra: above your belly button in your solar plexus region

Heart Chakra: your heart

Throat Chakra: located in your throat

Third Eye Chakra: on your forehead, slightly above eye level

Crown Chakra: located at the top of your head.

Gazing Meditation

Gazing, or Trataka Meditation, is when you fixate on an external object, such as a candle or perhaps an image or symbol. First you focus on the object with open eyes and then you close your eyes and visualize the object. This practice is meant to strengthen your powers of visualization and concentration.

Kriya Meditation

Kriya Yoga is a series of energy, breath and meditation exercises practiced by Paramahansa Yogananda. It is most often practiced for those who are seeking to practice the devotional and spiritual aspects of mediation.

Third Eye Meditation

Third Eye Meditation focuses on the 7th Chakra, or third eye (the area on the forehead between the eyes). All focus is centered toward this chakra to silence the mind.

Sound Meditation, or Nada Yoga

Sound Meditation focuses on sounds, both external and internal. You would begin with an external sound, perhaps calming music or nature sounds and focus all of your attention on the sound to quiet the mind. Then you would move to focusing on the internal sings of your mind and body.

Kundalini Meditation

Kundalini Meditation is extremely popular among wealthy individuals, especially celebrities. It is an extremely sophisticated and complex method of Yoga and should only be practiced with a licensed practitioner.

The goal of Kundalini Meditation is to awaken the "kundalini energy" at the Root Chakra (or base of your spine) as well as the awakening and development of your psychic energies with the end goal being completed spiritual enlightenment.

Pranayama

Pranayama is a method of regulated breathing. While it is not considered a meditation practice by most, it is a great way to calm the mind in preparation for yoga exercises or meditation practices. The most common techniques is the "4-4-4-4" method in which you would inhale, hold the breath, exhaled and relax for 4 second increments each. This practice can help calm the body and center the mind. It is beneficial as it can be practiced anytime and anywhere. It is a good method for those who suffer from anxiety or panic attacks.

Tantra Meditation

Tantra Meditation or Yoga, is not to be confused with "Tantric sex." Tantra Yoga is a very ancient practice that encompasses thousands of meditations, or mantras. Tantra Meditation is an extremely advanced form of yoga or meditation and is most often taught individually by a licensed practitioner.

As you can see, Yoga is an extremely diverse form of meditation. It can be practiced individually, and in its purest form, or it can be taught by a licensed professional and can be extremely complex, and even dangerous when not carried out properly.

Chinese Meditation

Chinese Meditation is different from other types of meditation in that it focuses on achieving wisdom through mediation. Its main purpose is to bring the mind to a higher state of awareness that result in a higher form of wisdom, knowledge and control over the mind, body and spirit.

Chinese Meditation has been around for ages, but has only become increasingly popular in the last few decades. It focuses on the body and the mind becoming one through deliberation. The ultimate goal of Chinese Meditation is to become a fully wise and wholly complete person that is fully aware of their purpose in life and of the world around them. It is the knowledge of both self-discovery and of the wisdom of the world around you.

Chi Kung Meditation (Qigong Meditation)

Chi Kung, or Qigong, Meditation is translated as "life energy cultivation." It is based on mind-body exercises for meditation as well as martial arts and health and fitness. It is based on regulated breathing, slower body movement and inner focus. Although it was practiced in China for thousands of years, it only recently becomes a worldwide sensation in the 20th century.

Chi Kung is practiced to relieve stress by channeling inner tranquility. It is believed to greatly reduce anger, stress, depression and even confusion as it brings total clarity to the mind. There are different exercises you can do while practicing Chi Kung. You can either find a licensed practitioner or there are plenty of tutorial videos online that detail the various body movements. Or you can simply focus on your breathing, as demonstrated in our brief "how to" guide below.

How to Practice Chi Kung Meditation

Choose a quiet, comfortable place where you will not be distracted. Choose your meditation position. Regulate your breathing.

In Chi Kung Meditation, your breathing pattern directly affects the quality of your meditation. You should breath in a pattern so that your breath is smooth, like calming waves. Do not rush your breathing, nor force it.

Example: Inhale for 6 count, hold for 3, exhale for 6, hold for 2, repeat. If you feel short of breath, take a break and then start again. This will become easier with practice. Then gradually increase the pattern by 2 second increments. Focus on this breathing pattern for ten minutes before returning to normal breathing. Clear Your Mind Settle your mind, clear all thoughts. If your focus is unclear, your energy will be scattered as well. Calm your mind and let the silence overtake you. Focus on your breathing, let your thoughts penetrate your mind, but do not focus on them, rather focus on your breathing. In time, your mind will settle.

Focus your attention on the center gravity of your body

This is also called the "lower dantian" which is about 2 inches above your belly button.

Allow the "QI" or energy to flow through your body, helping you achieve inner peace and clarity.

Taoism

Taoism dates back to 6th century BC and is both a religion and a philosophy. The main emphasis of Taoism is to live in complete harmony with Nature (Tao). The main doctrine of Taoism is the Tao Te Ching. The purpose of Taoism is to generate, transform and circulate your inner energy by quieting the mind and body, achieving inner peace and ultimately harmony with the Tao. Taoism has many different types of mediation. There are even some practices that focus solely on longevity and health.

Types of Taoism

Breathing Meditation (Zhuanqi)

This form of Taoism focuses on breathing in order to unite the mind and "qi." Your breathing gradually comes soft as you achieve the highest state of relaxation.

Emptiness Meditation

In this form of meditation, you will sit quietly and empty your mind of all mental images including all feelings, desires, thoughts, etc to achieve inner peace. The goal is to quiet the spirit and mind and become one with oneself and nature.

Neiguan

Neiguan Taoism is the practice of observing "inner vision", or the inside of your mind and body, to experience the "qi" and thought processes. In this practice you are becoming connected with the nature and wisdom of your body and your "inner being."

Taoism is best learned from an instructor, although there are many books, online videos and courses available. It is best practiced by those who enjoy nature and philosophy and want to get in touch with the natural world, as well as achieve inner peace and tranquility.

Christian Meditation

In the majority of religions or practices, meditation is practiced in order to obtain enlightenment. However, in some branches of Christianity, the goal of meditation is more contemplative with the goal being to form a closer relationship with the Trinity (Father, Son and Holy Spirit) or to gain a deeper understanding of the Bible. Some forms of Christianity, the more fundamentalist, traditional forms, frown upon meditation altogether, but today many branches of Christianity are accepting mediation as a form of contemplation prayer, higher spirituality or intimacy with God.

Types of Christian Meditation

Contemplative Reading

Contemplative Reading involves focusing on a passage or teaching of the Bible

Contemplative Prayer

Contemplative Prayer involves focus on devotions, with the silent repetition of a prayer or request.

Sitting with God

This is a silent form of meditation, usually after a teaching or reading, in which you would silence your mind and focus your mind, soul and heart solely on God and sit in His presence.

Guided Meditation

Guided Meditation is a relatively new form of mediation. It is becoming increasingly popular as our lives are becoming quite hectic these days.

Guided Meditation does, however, require a level of self-discipline. It is done via digital or audio media so it does take focus and discipline. It is also a good place to start practicing meditation.

Once you feel comfortable with guided meditation, you can then proceed to the next "level" in the meditation practice of your choice. The media is solely to guide you, hence the name "Guided meditation." It is strictly a personal journey so you need to be committed and serious.

Guided Meditation is usually paired with a cassette, DVD, CD or even a video. Guided meditation is a great place to start if you are new to the art of meditation or if you are having trouble with the more traditional forms of meditation.

Types of Guided Meditation

Binaural Beats

Binaural Beats were founded as a meditation practice by a physicist named Heinrich Wilhelm Dove in 1839. He basically determined that when two signals with different frequencies were present separately, one in each ear, the brain will detect the variations between the two frequencies and reconcile the difference. These binaural beats are believed to help increase concentration, boost energy and have a general calming feeling. They can be played on their own or with music. They have become increasing popular in recent years.

Relaxation and Body Scans

Relaxation and Body Scans help you reach a state of deep relaxation for your entire body. They are usually accompanied by nature sounds or relaxing instrumental music. You would focus on relaxing one area of the body at a time until you are completely relaxed and at ease. These are a good method of reducing anxiety and also aiding those with insomnia or sleep issues to achieve a state of deep sleep.

Traditional Meditations

These guided meditations simply use the instructor's voice to illustrate or "guide" you through the meditation (as the name suggests). These are often a brief tutorial followed by silence. They are very good for beginners.

Guided Imagery

Guided Imagery puts the powers of visualization and the imagination to use. The instructor's voice will guide you to picture an image, scene, object, etc. Guided imagery is used for relaxation or healing purposes.

Affirmations

Affirmations are usually paired with either relaxation or guided imagery, or both. The purpose is to place a positive message in your mind permanently to rid yourself of negative thoughts and feelings.

Conclusion

As you can see, there are many forms of meditation. Everyone is different so you need to find the type of meditation that works best for you. It might take some trial and error before you find the meditation practice that best fits your personality and lifestyle. You can choose to take a course with an instructor, join a yoga class or practice meditation on your own. Again this is an extremely personal decision as this is your journey and yours alone!

Chapter Four: Mindfulness & Meditation: How to practice mindfulness in every aspect of your everyday life

In the last chapter we touched briefly on Mindfulness Meditation. Essentially, the goal of Mindfulness Meditation is to bring our focus to the "here and now" rather than be distracted by the events and stressors of everyday life. In this chapter we shall go into further detail on how to practice mindfulness in every aspect of your everyday life.

We will use the terms "Mindfulness Meditation," "Lovingkindness Meditation" and "Metta Meditation" interchangeably as they are all closely related. In practicing mindfulness as a part of your daily life, you can easily obtain a sense of loving kindness, which will easily flow into every aspect of your life.

Mindfulness is often used in the workplace as well as by teachers, sports coaches, life coaches, psychologists and teachers to teach people how to focus on the present. Mindfulness can lead to peace of mind, happiness, decreased anxiety and depression and increased levels of concentration. The goal of mindfulness meditation is better physical, mental, spiritual, psychological and emotional health.

Ultimately, we can practice mindfulness in everything we do: whether we are walking, driving to work, cooking dinner, showering, playing with our children...wherever!

Why do we need mindfulness in everyday life?

Mindfulness can teach us to be mindful in every aspect of our lives. We can show more empathy, kindness and compassion for the world around us. We can be kinder to ourselves and gentler to ourselves. We are our own worst enemy.
We can be really harsh on ourselves and sometimes we let the negativity and bad thoughts overpower us. Mindfulness can help us counteract and filter out those negative thoughts so we can stay focused on the present moment.

We cannot love others unless we love ourselves. Cliché, but true. If we are angry and bitter about our lives, it will reflect in our thoughts, words and actions. If we don't treat ourselves with loving kindness, how can we possibly treat others the same? We need to start from the inside and let lovingkindness take over. Only then can we give others the love and respect they truly deserve.

If we go around constantly finding fault in others and the world around us, we cannot be a light to others. Negativity can hold us back from so much in life. Mindfulness can help us to overcome this negativity and to stop dwelling on the past and worrying about the future.

Think about it. Yes, we may have made mistakes in the past, but no one can go back and change the past, nor can we predict the future. That's why it is important to live in the "here and now." And this is what Mindfulness meditation helps us to do.

And on the same token, negativity can affect our mindfulness meditation. If we lose sight of our loving kindness and don't carry it with us through everyday life, we cannot fully focus on our Metta Meditation.

In the next section, we will discuss the "dimensions" of metta meditation and how to apply them to everyday life.

Stages of Mindfulness

The practice of metta meditation is based on four separate steps, or practices, called "Sublime Abodes." Each of these is an emotional state that we must experience in order to reach lovingkindness so that it can positively affect our lives.

Stage 1: Empathetic Joy (Mudita)

Mudita or Empathic Joy is the first state of mindfulness that we need to experience. This stage involves the happiness of others. When our mindfulness is "aware" of an other's happiness, it shifts our "feeling" tone. This is referred to as "empathic joy" (mudita) When we are happy for another's happiness, we experience a joy that puts us on their level. We can then in essence be happy simply because someone else is happy.

How many times, realistically, have we been at a negative point in our lives where another person's happiness just made us even more bitter? Mudita can help us overcome this. Instead of resenting another's happiness, we can experience true and genuine happiness for them. Empathetic Joy is unconditional joy. We are not happy for someone because we hope to gain from their happiness, we are happy because we enjoy seeing those we care about experience happiness.

Stage 2: Compassion (Karuna)

Compassion, or Karuna, is the stage of suffering. When our mindfulness is aware of suffering, it is transformed into compassion instead of sorrow, pain or anguish.

Compassion is the awareness of suffering and the meeting of mindfulness. It is another form of empathy, but it is more of a murting state in which we feel love and care for someone who is suffering, rather than sorrow, anger, bitterness, or even pity.

Stage 3: Equanimity (Upekkha)

Equanimity or Upekkha, is the stage of mindfulness in which we combine the nature of both suffering and joy.
At this stage we are able to sense the suffering and joy of others and see how these affect their actions. It is not a state of indifference, as one might suspect, it is a feeling of calm awareness, and acceptance, of others feelings. We become aware that these feelings exist in those around us, and we accept that those feelings are genuinely what that person is experiencing at that moment. In a sense we are letting them own their feelings and accepting the fact that they are feeling this way. We love and accept them regardless if they are experiencing joy, pain, anguish or sorrow.

Dimensions of Mindfulness

Sati (Recollection)

Sati is the dimension of mindfulness that aware of the present moment. For example, it is the awareness of our particular mood or state of mind at that particular time. We can determine if if mind is focuses or absent minded, we can focus on our posture, our breathing, our current emotions. We are mindful of every sensation that our body is experiencing, every thought that occurs and every emotion that we are currently experiencing. Sati is what we refer to as "being in the moment."

We need to be able to experience this state in order to make any meaningful decisions or changes in our lives. We will never be able to make any progress if we do not know where we are in the present moment.

Sampajañña

Sampajañña is the dimension in lovingkindness that follows over time. It gives us a sense and awareness of "purpose" (where we want to go) as well as an awareness of our "past" (where we have been). In this aspect of mindfulness, we are focusing on the future. Once we have a sense of where we want to go and what we want to achieve, we can then keep ourselves "in check" to make we are on the right track.

This can help us stay more focused in the present moment. It can help us focus on our progress in lovingkindness or in other words "Am I making a difference at the moment? Am I showing lovingkindness in the present moment?"

Sampajañña is also a means of reflection. It teaches us to recall the events of our day in a mindful way. We can analyze our "lapses" in mindfulness. Did we fail to practice mindfulness at any point of the day? How can we remedy this so it does not happen again? Sampajañña is necessary as it helps us to compare and contrast where we are going to where we want to be.

Dhamma-vicaya

Dhamma-Vicaya is the dimension of mindfulness that helps us to mentally compare the positive and negative aspects, or distractions, of our present state. In a sense, we are separating the negative from the positive. For example, we would categorize those "positive" aspects such as confidence, love, empathy, compassion and sort them from the "negative" or destructive aspects such as criticism, bitterness or anger.

In essence, Dhamma-Vicaya is a diagnostic measure, which lets us evaluate exactly what is happening. We make a mental list of the "pros and cons" of our current state and analyze those feelings so we can get past them and focus on the "here and now" rather than the emotions, positive or negative, that can hold us back.

Appamada

Appamada is the dimension of mindfulness that is focused on "vigilance" or watchfulness. It is the state of mindfulness that fully focuses on the importance of the task at hand at that moment. These four dimensions of mindfulness work together. We must develop them separately while at the same time they must work together. They are not always easy to separate so we must learn to use them both independently and dependently.

This may seem a bit overwhelming. Let's try to put it simply. If you are aware of your present state of mind, while at the same time aware that there is something hindering you from moving forward and if you are vigilantly pulling yourself back to the present moment, then all of the dimensions of mindfulness are present. It might seem like a lot, but the more you practice, the easier it will be.

Understanding the four dimensions of loving kindness can make our lives so much easier. If we don't have the ability to "name" our current mental state, then we will not be able to move ahead, let alone focus on the present moment. Taking the time to experience these dimensions of mindfulness will go a long way in achieving a permanent state of mindfulness.

You are probably feeling a bit shell-shocked right now. This is a lot to process. You need to not only familiarize yourself with the 3 stages of mindfulness, now you need to be able to experience each of the four dimensions as well. Don't let this discourage you. It will take time and lots of practice. And a great deal of self-reflection and introspection. You might find that you can easily achieve compassion and empathic joy but you have trouble achieving equanimity. Or you may be able to easily separate the negative from the positive (dhamma-vicaya) but have trouble staying focused on the present moment (appamada) everyone is different.

We all have our strengths and weaknesses. Don't let this deter you from achieving mindfulness. We are not giving you this information to scare you, or to make you feel overwhelmed. We are simply giving you the information on the stages and dimensions of mindfulness so that you will have a basic understanding of what mindfulness fully entails.

It might seem like a lot, but when once you start to practice mindfulness meditation, these things become second nature.

Now that we have given you the linguists of mindfulness, let us give you some pointers on how to practice mindfulness in everyday life. This is where it gets easier, so relax! Why not try some of the breathing exercises we discussed in Chapter 3?

Top tips how to practice mindfulness in everyday Life

In Chapter Two, when we discussed the types of meditation, we outlined the steps of how to practice mindfulness meditation. Now we are going to show you ways in which you can carry that feeling of loving kindness with you wherever you go. These tips will help you practice mindfulness throughout your day. Not every tip will suit you, but this is just a guideline to help you work mindfulness into your daily routine.

Practice mindfulness from the moment you open your eyes

If you practice mindfulness from the moment you first wake up, it sets the "tone" for the day. Once you are in the right mindset, it will become easier to make mindfulness a part of your everyday routine.

Don't reach for your cell phone the second you open your eyes, practice mindfulness instead.

Don't turn on the tv, check your social media sites or answer texts or emails, but make mindfulness your first priority, before you even put your feet on the floor. Getting an early start can make or break your day.

Practice mindfulness during your "mundane" routine activities
There are things we do on autopilot, such as dress, shower, make coffee, eat our breakfast.

These are all ideal times to focus on mindfulness. Be fully aware of what you are feeling at each moment. How does the water feel in the shower? How does your coffee taste? What are you feeling as you dress for work? These simple, everyday tasks are a great way to practice mindfulness and to keep you focused on the "here and now."

Practice mindfulness while you wait
We all lead busy lives, but there are moments while we are "waiting" whether we are stuck in traffic, waiting for the bus or train on the commute to work, waiting in line at the bank, and so forth. Use these moments to practice mindfulness.

It can help reduce the doldrums of waiting and before you know it, the time has passed!

Don't let the stages and dimensions throw you off. Once you are able to easily tell the difference between each, they will become second nature. As you are consciously practicing mindfulness as you go through your day, it will become easier. You will feel connected to the moment and the world around you. Once you are mindful of your feelings, thoughts and surroundings, loving kindness will flow naturally and you will feel more at peace than you ever have before

Chapter Five: Conclusion & Appendixes

We just threw a great deal of information your way! So if you feel a bit intimidated, it's okay. Take a deep breath and relax! The purpose of this book was to give you an overview into the history, practice and benefits of meditation, as well as to offer you some additional tips and insight.

Remember to choose the form of meditation that works best for you. What works for your sister or your co-worker might not be the best fit for your like. Use trial and error. If you find that one form of meditation is not working for you, then try another.

Have fun with it! Make it a challenge and make it a part of your daily routine. Before you know it, you'll be a pro! Congratulations for deciding to undertake the time-honored tradition of meditation and good luck!

Appendix 1: Glossary of Terms Most Frequently Used in Meditation

The following is a list of some of the most commonly used words, terms and phrases in the art of meditation.

Ashram: spiritual community in which the focus is on meditation and spiritual living

Buddha: Buddha is the term for the "enlightened one", in meditation the term "Buddha" refers to Siddhartha Gautama, the spiritual leader in ancient India who is believed to be the founder of Tantric or Buddhist meditation.

Chakra: the chakra is the "energy center" which consists of 7 areas: the root, the sacrum, the solar plexus, the heart, the throat, the third eye and the crown. Each chakra is associated with an element, color, or symbol and a specific significance.

Dharma: the teachings of Buddha, specifically Siddhartha Gautama, often referred to as the "truth" or the "path of truth"

Enlightenment: the "attainment" of reaching full spiritual awakeness or spiritual awakening, also referred to as "nirvana"

Mantra: a series of words, sounds, or a phase that is used in meditation to reach a higher level of consciousness

Metta (Maitri): Loving kindness

Mala: strand of 108 beads often used in Mantra and other meditation practices to keep count of the number of times the mantra has been repeated/chanted.

Mindfulness: the ability to, or practice of, paying full attention to the moment or situation at hand.

Nirvana: the ultimate state of complete and total enlightenment. This is only achieved when one experiences a true sense of stillness and peace of mind once all other obstacles have been removed.

Shamatha: "Calm abiding" breathing technique, most often used in mindful breathing

Zafu: circular pillow used for meditation practices involving sitting or kneeling

Zen: a theory, or school, of Buddhism which centers enlightenment as its main goal.

Appendix 2: Common Mantras Used In Meditation

These are just a few of the most popular and traditional mantras that are most commonly used in practicing meditation. Of course you can use your own something as simple as "Today I will embody love, peace and harmony." Or whatever you chose. Again, if you are studying with a meditation or yoga practitioner, especially in Transcendental Meditation, they may give you your own personal mantra. Again, a mantra is an extremely personal thing. Choose a mantra that works best for you and with which you feel comfortable. And don't worry, over time, it will become much easier as it becomes a part of you!

Om: (Sanskrit/Hindu) Translation: "It is" or "To Become" This is the most common and sacred mantra in history.

Om Mani Padme Hum: (Buddhist) Translation: "Hail the Jewel in the Lotus (aka Buddah)

Ham-Sah (So Ham) (Sanskrit) Translation: "I am THAT"

Om Namah Shivaya (Hindu) Translation: "I bow to Shiva"

El Shaddai (Hebrew) Translation: God Almighty
Elohim (Hebrew) Translation: Hebrew name of God

Maranatha (Hebrew) Translation: Come, Lord, Come

Sat, Chit, Ananda (Sanskrit) Translation: Existence. Consciousness. Bliss

Appendix 3: Top tips for practicing meditation

We couldn't leave you without some helpful hints on how to practice meditation. Again, this is a general guide. Not every tip will work for you, but these should give you a basic guide on how to practice meditation as part of your daily routine.

Make it a part of your daily routine

If you are truly serious about meditation, you should practice every day. If you are a morning person, make it a part of your morning routine. Or if you are using meditation to help you rewind, relax and reflect on your day, make it a part of your nightly routine, perhaps just before going to sleep. Or both, if that's what you want.

But if you really want to make meditation work for you, you need to seriously practice it regularly, not just on occasion. You can even set a personal reminder for yourself in your phone so you won't forget if you've had an extremely hectic day (which is usually when you need to meditate the most)

Start slowly

If you are new to meditation and have a short attention span, you might want to ease yourself gradually into your routine. Start with a five-minute meditation and work your way up. This way you won't feel overwhelmed and you won't be berating yourself if you can't meditate for 45 minutes straightaway.

Don't get too caught up on technique

If you are someone who is perhaps were structured and regimented than perhaps technique is a big deal to you. You want to ensure that you are doing everything according to "textbook."

Don't take yourself too seriously and don't be hard on yourself if you don't have it down pat right away. It's going to take some time. Take baby steps. Maybe work on your posture for the first week, then the next week focus on your breathing and so forth. Take your time and it will all fall into place eventually.

Count your breaths

Again start small, you are essentially "training" your body and your mind. Start with counting "one" as you inhale and "two" as you exhale and gradually increase your count as you get more experienced and feel more comfortable. Again, with practice, this will all become second nature.

Refocus when your mind wanders

Unless you already have supernatural powers of concentration, your mind is going to wander at first. Don't get discouraged. Acknowledge and accept your thoughts and then refocus and recenter. You are human, not a supernatural mystic being. It's going to take time before you can completely "empty" your mind.

Don't worry if you can't completely "clear" your mind

Again, don't let yourself get stressed if your mind wanders. Maybe the thing that keeps popping into your head is something you need to put your focus on. Again, never totally dismiss your thoughts. They are a part of you, accept them and move on.

Go with the flow

One of the purposes of meditation is to teach our minds and bodies to relax and be more loving and accepting. If your mind keeps wandering back to a certain topic, then maybe that is where your focus should be at the moment. If you find yourself "lost in a moment" or a piece of music or a teaching that wasn't part of your "plan" for that specific mediation, go with it! You never know what you might discover in the process

PRACTICE! PRACTICE! PRACTICE!!

We cannot stress this enough! You are not going to be an expert overnight. It can take years to become fully "spiritually enlightened." (if this in fact, is your ultimate goal) Whatever your goal, don't get discouraged and don't give up. The old adage is true: "Practice makes perfect." The more you practice your meditation techniques, the easier they will become.

Do not meditate right after a meal

Meditating on a full stomach can tend to make you feel sleepy, or even cause indigestion. Let your food digest a bit before sitting down for an extended period of time.

On the same hand, you don't want to meditate on an empty stomach either or you won't be able to focus and may even feel weak.

Stay hydrated

Drinking water is crucial in so many aspects of our lives. If you are going to be sitting for a long period of time it is important that your body is properly hydrated so you don't become lightheaded. You don't want to drink a full gallon of water immediately before meditating, but you want to make sure that you are properly hydrated before you begin.

Eliminate all distractions

Unless you absolutely need to have your cell phone handy (if you are a parent, etc), you should turn off your phone or keep it on silent. Find a place where you will not be distracted from the noises of everyday life (tv, radio, other people, etc). The less distracted you are, the easier it will be to meditate.

Find a support network

Join a glass or a group. It is always easier to start something new and keep at it if you have encouragement. If you don't have time to join a class, or you want to practice strictly solo, you can always find online support groups and forums for advice and encouragement.

It's not a competition

You are not in competition with anyone, this is not a race, it is a personal journey. Also don't be too hard on yourself. Everyone works at their own pace. Enjoy the journey and don't get so caught up on technique, etc, that you aren't benefiting from the experience. Meditation is a learning process. Be kind and loving to yourself along the way.

Use the restroom before you meditate

This should be a no-brainer, but sometimes we get caught up in our routines and forget. Try to use the facilities before you meditate so you will not have to stop halfway through your mediation to run to the restroom. This is especially helpful if you are planning on doing a walking meditation or you are meditating somewhere in nature.

Experiment

Experiment with different types of meditation until you find the one that works best for you. If you try Zen meditation and discover that it is not for you, don't give up. There are plenty of other meditation techniques available. Practice trial and error until you find the form of meditation that best works for you.

Get up slowly

Never jump right up or stand up too quickly after meditating, especially after a particularly long meditation. Stretch your arms and get up slowly. Stretch some more. You need to get your blood circulating again. Standing too quickly can cause you to feel lightheaded, become dizzy and even lose your balance.

Keep an open mind

Rid yourself of all preconceived notions about meditation. Let go of all negative and judgmental thoughts. Keep your mind open and embrace your experiences. Relax and enjoy it and it will make your journey more enjoyable and rewarding. You just might learn something new about yourself!

Be aware of your body

The point of meditation is to discover things about yourself and the world around you. Pay attention to what your body is telling you. Focus on that thought or feeling. Our bodies send us messages and sometimes we are so caught up in our lives that we ignore these signals. Use these feelings as a guide in your practice. Part of mindfulness is to become fully aware of our bodies and minds so pay attention to what your body is trying to tell you!

Mediate with others

If you feel comfortable enough to "share" your meditation time with others, it could be a very rewarding experience. Invite your best friend, sibling, or significant other. However, if you do not feel comfortable doing so, that is your decisions. Meditation practice is a very personal issue and it is up to you when and if you decided to share that experience with someone else. Never do anything that makes you feel unsafe!

Set a timer

If you are on a set schedule, it might be a good idea to set a timer so you don't lose track of time. You don't have to do this, it is entirely up to you, but if you have an appointment, or need to pick your children up from school or something, there is nothing wrong with setting a timer so you don't lose track of time!

Appendix Four: References

"A Handy Guide to 24 Common Meditation Terms. | elephant journal." 2013. 12 May. 2016 <http://www.elephantjournal.com/2013/12/a-quick-guide-to-24-common-meditation-terms>

"History of Meditation - Best Healing Meditation Online." 2012. 12 May. 2016 <http://besthealingmeditationonline.com/meditation/history-of-meditation/>

"History Of Meditation | Meditation Techniques." 2011. 12 May. 2016 <http://24x7meditation.blogspot.com/2011/09/history-of-meditation-where-did.html>

"Meditation provides physical, mental, and emotional benefits." 2011. 12 May. 2016 <http://www.humankinetics.com/excerpts/excerpts/meditation-provides-physical-mental-and-emotional-benefits>

"Benefits of Meditation | The Art of Living." 2015. 12 May. 2016 <http://www.artofliving.org/us-en/meditation/meditation-for-you/benefits-of-meditation>

Yoga, R. "Physical and health benefits of meditation - Ananda Palo Alto." 2007. <http://www.anandapaloalto.org/joy/BenefitsOfMeditation.html>

23 Types of Meditation - Find The Best Techniques ... - Live and Dare." 2015. 12 May. 2016 <http://liveanddare.com/types-of-meditation/>

"Loving-Kindness Meditation | The Center for Contemplative Mind in ..." 2012. 12 May. 2016 <http://www.contemplativemind.org/practices/tree/loving-kindness>

"Transcendental Meditation: Benefits, Technique, and More - WebMD." 2011. 12 May. 2016 <http://www.webmd.com/balance/guide/transcendental-meditation-benefits-technique>

"Beginner's Guide to Common Yoga Chants and ... - Yoga Journal." 2014. 12 May. 2016 <http://www.yogajournal.com/article/lifestyle/the-beginner-s-guide-to-common-chants/>

"The 7 Chakras - A Beginners Guide To Your Energy System | Zenlama." 2013. 12 May. 2016 <http://www.zenlama.com/the-7-chakras-a-beginners-guide-to-your-energy-system/>

"Mindfulness: Getting Started - Mindful." 2015. 12 May. 2016 <http://www.mindful.org/meditation/mindfulness-getting-started/>

"Mindfulness in Daily Life — Blue Cliff Monastery." 2015. 12 May. 2016 <http://www.bluecliffmonastery.org/be-mindful-in-daily-life/>

"Lovingkindness meditation | Wildmind Buddhist Meditation." 2007. 12 May. 2016 <http://www.wildmind.org/metta>

18480149R00058

Printed in Great Britain
by Amazon